Echoes & Visions

To Bro. Anthony Starks
May you be Blessed
abundantly
    Ameena H. Ahmad
    3-20-01

Echoes & Visions

Reflections on a Life of Poetry

Ameerah Hasin Ahmad

To my parents
Mr. Raymond P. Hall and
Mrs. Mae P. Hall
Much love and appreciation to my children Talib,
Muslimah, Musaddiq, Kalimah and Luqman

Echoes & Visions: A Reflection on A Life of Poetry. All rights reserved. No part of this book may be reproduced or duplicated in any way or incorporated in any commercial programs, books, databases or stored in any retrieval systems or transmitted in any form, by any means, including mechanical, electronic, photo-copying, recording without the express written consent of the publisher, except in the form of brief excerpts or quotations for the purpose of a review. The material contained herein are for the personal use of the reader and may not be used other wise.

COVER PHOTO:*Artoni*
GARMENT DESIGN: MADINAH BILAL

Library of Congress Cataloging-in-Publication Data

Ameerah Hasin Ahmad
(201) 860-6888

First printing
97 98 99 00 01 6 5 4 3 2 1

Manufactured and Printed in the United States

CONTENTS

Part One: Community

Poet Tree 10
Mommy Mae and Poppa Ray 11
Community 12
Heritage 13
Double Dutch Sister 14
Take It To The Hoop 16
My Little Brother 18
Ya Think Ya Grown 20
Stigma 21
Dignified Woman 22
Keep The Dream Alive 23
Woman So Beautiful 25
The Sun Rose In South Africa 26
Somali Rose 27
The Elder 28
Sister Smile 29
Soul Vibrations 29
Home 30
Cardboard Beds 31
April 32
Main Line 34
$1.00 35
Milking The Money 36
Cracked Jars 37

Soul Liberation 38
Restraining Order 39
Some Call It Jazz....................... 40
The Wailing Of Robert Nesta Marley......... 41
He's My Drummer Brother
    (For My Brother Vincent Hall 44
The Brilliant Giant Paul Robeson 45
Billie Holiday 46
The Red Snow Of Sarajevo 48
This Trane............................ 50
The Burning Spear Guardian Of Reggae 51

Part two: Metamorphosis of Love
Path................................. 54
Honey Hush!.......................... 55
The Phone Started Ringing 57
Sunman.............................. 58
Our Friendship 60
Bouquet.............................. 61
Why 62
You 63

Part Three: Inner Visions
It's Later Than We Think 66
Gifts Among Myriads 68
Cherish 70
Dreams 70

Inner Vision	71
Truth	73
Joy Of Giving	73
As The Worm Turns	74
Patterns	75
Morning Glories	75
From Liberty Park	76
From The Beach	77
From The Mountain	77
From Negril	78
The Bird	79
Dance Of The Dandelions	80
21,000 Feet	80
Eyes Are Windows	81
A Reminder	81
Consolation	82
Autumn Again	82
Respect To The Max	83
New Beginnings	84
Usually After The Brainstorm	84
The Days	85
Winter	87
Ramadan Rapture	88
I'm Just A Poem	89
Water	90
May 19, 1996	91

COMMUNITY

Vanessa Holley

COME SIT UNDER MY POET TREE
POET TREE
COME SIT UNDER MY POET TREE
REST YOUR FEET
LISTEN TO ME
COME SIT UNDER MY POET TREE
POET TREE
COME SIT UNDER MY POET TREE
OPEN YOUR MIND
SET IT FREE
COME SIT UNDER MY POET TREE
POET TREE
COME SIT UNDER MY POET TREE

REST, RELAX

BE WITH ME

COME

SIT

UNDER

MY

POET TREE

FOR MY PARENTS
MOMMY MAE AND POPPA RAY

POPPA RAY
WHAT CAN I SAY
  I LOVE YOU
YOU WHO PUT
THE *S* IN SACRIFICE
AND THE *F* IN FAMILY
AND WHEN
YOU TOLD US ONCE
ONCE WAS ENOUGH
YOU DEAR FATHER
WHO WORKED
WHO TOILED
SO WE FOUR
COULD HAVE
YOU
WHO LOVED
PROVIDED
CONSISTENTLY
THERE
WHO TAUGHT
RECITED POEMS
OF LIFE
EXPERIENCE
AND ADVENTURE
YOU
WHO LET US
MAKE A CHOICE
AFTER THE FACTS
THEN ASKED
THE MAIN QUESTION
"WELL ARE YOU HAPPY?"
POPPA RAY
WHAT CAN I SAY
YOU
LAID BACK
SO COOL
QUIET
DEEP
A WISE MAN
AT TIMES JOVIAL
WILLING TO LIFT
SPIRITS FALLEN
HAPPY TO CELEBRATE
JOIN IN VICTORY
ALWAYS WILLING
TO BE A FRIEND
THANK YOU POPPA
BLESS YOU
FOR EVERYTHING

AND MOMMY MAE
WHAT CAN I SAY
  I LOVE YOU
IS WHAT
I LEARNED FROM YOU
YES YOU
WHO PUT THE *M* IN MOTHER
THE *L* IN LADY
TAUGHT US
SHOWED US
HOW CULTURE IS
ENJOYABLE
AND CRUCIAL
TO THE HEART
YOU MOTHER
WHO NURTURED
AND PROTECTED US
AND WHEN
YOU PUT YOUR EYE
ON SOMEONE
YOU READ THEM WELL
ALL FOR A LESSON
IN A TIME
WE WOULDN'T ADMIT
BUT YOU
WAITED, WATCHED
YES CALLED IT RIGHT
THEN WE GREW
WHILE YOU ALWAYS
KNEW AND PRAYED
TO YOUR SOURCE
MOMMY MAE
WHAT CAN I SAY
QUEEN OF ALL COOKS
SHARP AS A PIN
DANCIN WITH POPPA
TO LESTER YOUNG
MOVING TO
THE RHYTHM MOON
AND STARS
YES YOU
GAVE TO US
WHAT THE ANCESTORS
GAVE TO YOU
THE SPIRIT
THE LOVE OF MOTHER
THANK YOU MOMMY
BLESS YOU
FOR EVERYTHING

Community

> Come
> Unity
> Come
> Come unity come
> Community, community
> We each have to come
> Face to face
> Consider the time
> And find your place
> We each have to come
> Face to face
> Consider the time
> And get in the race
> Go inside the home
> > COMMUNITY!
> Go outside the door
> > COMMUNITY!
> Be divided no more
> > COMMUNITY!
> Go into the street
> > COMMUNITY!
> Truth to live
> > COMMUNITY!
> Truth to teach
> > COMMUNITY!
> Families to unite
> > COMMUNITY!
> People to greet
> > COMMUNITY!
> There's a world to remake
> > COMMUNITY!
> We've got to relate
> > COMMUNITY!
> Stay on the track
> > COMMUNITY!
> There's no turning back
> > COMMUNITY!
> Just consider the time
> > COMMUNITY!
> Let all the light shine
> > *COMMUNITY, UNITY,*
> > > *COMMUNITY UNITY*

HERITAGE

This heritage of mine
I dare not deny
A golden legacy
Forever held high

Echoes of our ancestors
A mighty glorious past
Echoes of the slavery
Into which my people were cast

This heritage of mine
Seeps into my deepest
Deepest dreams
Stirs within my soul
Even speaks
Through my genes

Telling me a story
Of a long weary trail
Pushing me
On to the victory
Destined to prevail

This heritage of mine
My roots
And the part I must play
Reflects in the fruits
Of a present
Future day

For I dare not expect many
To comprehend
The very essence
Of what I am

What I am, what I am
I am the African
African American.

DOUBLE DUTCH SISTER

Jump on little sister
With that skip and hop
And don't let that rope
Trip you up child
Be patient
Wait your turn
Now jump it
You've got to try
Little sister
Just a little split
With that kick
Now turn around
And don't you miss
A beat
When you tap that ground

And when
You have to hold your end
Hold it tight
Keep it even
Be fair
And turn it right
Be sure to tell them
How you want
Your rope to go
Hot pepper
Medium or slow

Community

You might be a beginner
You might be a winner
But keep those feet steady
Cause that rope
Sure can burn your leg
Sometimes
Jump it, kick it
See how high
The number can go
How long is that rap
Going to last
You can't tell sometimes
With a clappity rope
Especially when
Somebody's armpit is hurting
So what you have to do Is switch it my sister
Give the end to somebody else
And just keep on
Jumping on.

TAKE IT TO THE HOOP

They were calling all the shots
As you ran down the court
Sweating
Just betting you would fail
To achieve your goal

Psyche! Then take it to the hoop Slamdunk, Shoot!

You came from a generation
Of achievers, leaders
Who were deliberately shoved
Then locked out of bounds
So grab that ball

Jump up Take it to the hoop Slamdunk, Shoot!

Seize the moment
Snatch the opportunity
You know it's your time
Even at the foul line
You know it's your time
All you have to do
Is use all those fancy moves
That come so naturally
To you
Then take it
Dribble it
Straight up
To the victory
If by chance you miss
Don't get pissed

Snatch it Take it to the hoop Slamdunk, Shoot!

Community

You see
They gave you
A negative label to wear
Then set you up
With the play
Drew the lines
Boundaries
That confined your mind
Now that you know
The Truth
The ball is in
Your court
Get up! Jump up!

Take it to the hoop Slamdunk, shoot!

MY LITTLE BROTHER

He plays in the lots
There in the shadow
Of abandoned buildings
Dreaming of far away lands

He plays
He runs
He flips
Like an Olympic star
On a urine soaked mattress
He jumps
He flies
Right through school bells
Right through meals

He plays and plays
Rolling the burnt rubber tire
Through broken snapple bottles
Which he pretends
Are bowling pins

He creates his fun
From what is available to him
And if he should get bored
With this game
Then right over there
Lying in the chromium soil
Among rusty nails
Used condoms
Needles
Glass
Dead cats
Chicken bones

Community

And trash
Are hundreds
Of empty glass viles
With which he can play marbles
Or perhaps
He can release his energy
By throwing rocks
Against the glass windows
Where he sees a reflection
Of the adult world
Which abandoned him

YA THINK YA GROWN

Ya think ya grown
But Momma knows
Changed your diapers
Washed you clean
From your head
Down to your toes

Ya think ya grown
But Momma knows
Dried your tears
Wiped the snot
From your nose

So
Ya better not
Ever forget
No matter how big
Or tall
Ya might get

No
Ya ain't there
Yet
Momma knows
Momma knows

Her hand
Was the hand
Held you
So tight
Loved you
Rocked you
Watched you
Day and night

Ya think ya grown
But momma knows
Momma knows.

STIGMA

That's not my coat
That's not my size
Not even my taste
Or style
Uh uh
Never
Shall I wear it
Or live down
To the purpose
For which It was designed
No, uh uh
Never
Shall I accept it
Or bear the burden
Of it's ugly fashion
Never
Shall I promote it
That's not my coat
Uh uh
Not even my style
Don't put it on me
Or ask me
To try it on -
For no alterations
Will make it fit me
Read my lips
No thank you!

DIGNIFIED WOMAN

Like a cultured pearl
Polished
Refined
You come from a place
Deeper than the ocean
You go far pass
A physical appearance
The crown
Covering your knowledge
Sparkles with radiance
Designed only
For your head
Which you hold high
Proud and humble
Your stride graceful
Beautiful
Through the time
That formed you
Walk tall my sister
Your very essence
Yields priceless jewels
Your eyes
Like cups
Carry water of wisdom
And love
Your tongue
Speaks words
Pregnant with the life
You've tasted
Walk tall my sister
Walk tall
Dignified Lady
Your heart
Like a womb
Holds the faith
The truth
Which bathes
Then guides your feet
Walk tall
Dignified Woman
Dignified Woman
Walk tall

KEEP THE DREAM ALIVE

Keep the dream alive
On Martin Luther King Drive
Coretta might visit
Who?
Have we forgotten?
Mud has collected
On street signs
Bearing Martin's name

Peace did not come
Freedom did not come
When it changed
From Jackson Avenue
Pacification did
Well
Some pride did
Some rights did

You say
"Power to the People"
We say
"Challenge to the People"
Keep the dream alive
On M.L.K. drive

They ask
"Where were you stabbed?"
M.L.K. Drive
"Where were you shot?"
M.L.K. Drive
"Where were you robbed?"
M.L.K. Drive
"And where are our babies?"
M.L.K. Drive
Bullets Flying
M.L.K. Drive

Squad cars speeding
Where
M.L.K. Drive

It's not an impossible dream
Nor
An unreachable mountain top
It's not a hopeless picture
But
A rewarding cause
Keep the dream alive
On M.L.K. Drive
So we all
May walk it"
And
        Truly be proud of it.

WOMAN SO BEAUTIFUL

Woman so beautiful
So beautiful to be
Womb of man
Womb of mind
A deeper meaning
For the world to see
Woman so beautiful
Not just in a physical way
God places in her care
The tender new life
To nourish from day to day
It's woman, womb of mind
So beautiful to be
The truth liberates her
In a just society
Woman is more
Than some physical flesh
More than a body
Behind a dress
Her nature, her mentality
Has great worth
Woman
A greater mission
On this earth.

THE SUN ROSE IN SOUTH AFRICA

A dark heavy cloud
Loitered above the land
Poured down Its polluted apartheid
An oppressive spirit
Resided within
Casted a hateful shadow
> BUT THE SUN STILL ROSE
> IN SOUTH AFRICA

Penetrating rays
Revealed the faces
Of cowardly beings
In whose hands
Were bullets and black books
> BUT THE SUN STILL ROSE
> IN SOUTH AFRICA

The dark gusting winds
Of hatred and greed
Blew across Capetown
Johannesburg
Soweto
Rolled, rumbled
Scattered tribes
Herded them like cattle
To reserved homelands
> BUT THE SUN STILL ROSE
> IN SOUTH AFRICA

And with it
Rose the people
Rose the vision
Rose the voice Of JUSTICE!

SOMALI ROSE

Suppose
You were like the rose
Copper brown petals
Open to the sun
Reaching toward light
Your large black eyes
Like a million black pearls
Millions of beautiful black pearls
Staring at the world
Suppose
You were the rose
Tears falling
Falling to the baked earth
Where your roots lay
Clinging, withering, searching
For compassion to feed on
A rose of nobility
Wounded
Drained of life's dew
Your seeds scattered
Across the hot dry desert
Your stems
Broken down to dust
Suppose
You were like the rose
THE SOMALI ROSE
Beautiful burnt copper brown
Petals open to the hope
That relief is the food
That will feed you
Your million black marble eyes
Staring, fixed
Calling to the love
Which must water you
Save you
Suppose
You were like the rose
Beautiful copper brown
Petals open
Like a bowl
Waiting to be filled.

THE ELDER

I have a question mark
In my eyes
Because the elder
Smiled about something
I don't yet realize

Why did you smile like that
Elder
What did you see
While I was talking
About my journey
And what's happening
With me

Why did you smile like that
Elder
While I was just as serious
As a heart attack

What is it you know
That I don't know
Oh
You say you told me
So
A long time ago

SISTER SMILE

Sister
When you smile
Your face glows
Like a big sunray
Of light
Because your heart
Is warm
And you have
Peace of mind
Sister
When you smile
You are just like
Sunshine
Why do you think
It reflects time
So sister
Keep smiling
Don't pout
You are beautiful
And you have something
Special to smile about

SOUL VIBRATIONS

Those that possess them
Know what to do with them
Leaving a lasting impression
A positive intuitive connection
Which there are
Just simply no words
To describe the feeling
The energy and spirit
Being thrown off by
And exchanged
Between soul people.

HOME

A place of warmth
Abode of peace
Where one can rest
And feel at ease
Something of your own
Or for those dear
You set the tone
Decide who enters there
A space to grow
In which to live
Where you can go
And be creative
Your special garden
Where you feel free
A loving room
Where you're Blessed to be

CARDBOARD BEDS

In the subways
The tunnels
The alleys
And the stations
They're just knocking
Kicking at the cellar door
Of a spoiled
And wasteful nation
  Tell me
  Where can I find
  A place to sleep
  A place to wash
  Or just a little
  Something to eat?
Just roamin
Roamin, roamin
Cryin, dyin
In the cold

Community

Cold hot street
With swollen ankles
And infected feet
Cardboard beds
Below their heads
Homeless
In a home
That is not their own
Homeless
In a home
Fit for rats alone
Where society's fallout
Pollutes the air
Then urinates down
Vapors of hopelessness
And despair
Relief
Only comes
With those who care
And hope
Lies within a prayer
Cardboard beds
Below their heads
Homeless
In a home
That is not their own
Homeless
In a home
Fit for rats alone
Tell me
Can you spare
Just one penny
I'm out here
Trying to make it In the land
Called "Good and Plenty"
Cardboard beds
Below their heads
Hungry in a land
Where even
Garbage cans eat bread.

APRIL

One in an icy December
April sat
In a public bathroom
Crouched beneath the sink
Dreaming of spring colors
To come
And paint her cheeks
Back to life
There April sat
Nervous, paranoid
Thin to the bone
Asking nothing yet waiting
Waiting for the vision
In her mind
To rescue her

As we shared hot cocoa
And a donut
I asked

"Why not the shelter"

She cringed
"They take your things
Do stuff to you
Bother you
It's safer here
My boyfriend is coming
He's coming back
To get me
To help me
He's coming back
She convinced herself

Community

So she stood before the mirror
Plaited two cornrows
Paced back and forth
Then sat
Waiting
Waiting for a new season

We parted friendly strangers
Many months passed
Until one steamy August
April was dancing
Dancing in the sunshine
Her face like a flower
Kissed by the joy of life
I stared from a distance
Smiling at her rebirth

MAIN LINE

Look better don't I?
Ain't doing all that stuff
I was doing before

Look better don't I?
See my eyes
Ain't they clear?

Can't you tell
Got myself together now

All I been doing lately
Is sleeping, sleeping
And sleeping
Getting a lot of rest
That's all
Look better don't I

Ain't getting high no more
Don't I look better
Tell the truth

Just been
Resting, resting
And resting

Hey
Say looka here
Do me a little favor
Can you lend me
A couple of dollars
Just two
Five
Well ten then
I pay you back
Swear
I pay you back
When my money
Comes in

Yeah Look better don't I?

Community

$1.00

*C*ome, see, look!
I give you good price
I give you good price
A good good price
Best price
Come, see, look
$1.00, $1.00, $1.00!
Red, blue, green pacifier
Pins $1.00
X pin $1.00
Michael Jackson $1.00
Michael Jordan $1.00
Everything, everything
$ 1 . 00
Magic $1.00
Barney sticker $1.00
Tell mudda
Tell fadda
Come see, look
$1.00, $1.00, $1.00
Gold tooth
More dollar
Gold chain
Many, many dollar
I give you good price
Yes good price
See fake one
Like real
$ 1 . 00
Hey come see
$1.00,$1.00, $1.00
Everything need go
Red blue, green pacifier
Just one dollar
Thank-you
Come back
Tell friend
$ 1 . 00

MILKING THE MONEY

One day I came across these laborers
You see
They were working
You know what I'm saying
Sweating
You know what I'm saying
Scheming
You know what I'm saying
They were just tricking
For the money
Milking people
While hosting them
And treating them
Like sweet honey
But they were only
Working you see
And playing a game
You know what I'm saying
Forgetting their name
While the game
Was being played on them
But I knew
It had nothing to do
With PEACE, LOVE, UNITY
Or being a friend
You know what I'm saying
They were just working
Milking
You see
Milking the money
Just milking the money
Over and over again.

CRACKED JARS

I haven't snapped
I said
I haven't snapped
All the peanut butter jars
Are cracked
They can recall
Recycle, remold
Reseal, reinspect
And resell them
They still come out
Cracked jars
With missing labels
From Skippy
To Peter Pan
Jiffy, Smuckers
And that new brand
Super Man
All cracked
Because
They don't read
GEORGE WASHINGTON CARVER
SCIENTIST
INVENTOR
Of creamy
Crunchy peanut butter

SOUL LIBERATION

People talk
Talk about liberation
Talk about freedom
Talk about justice
Talk about truth
Talk about change
Talk about unity
Talk about peace

But what we need
Is real solidarity
Between sisters
And brothers
The Inner change
The natural
The spiritual
Freedom from
A negative mentality
A negative life
Freedom from
Negative expression
People talk
Talk about rights
We need
INNER REVOLUTION
Heart, mind and soul
People talk
Talk about freedom
Talk about progress
Talk about respect
All that's good
But what we need
Is a SOUL LIBERATION.

RESTRAINING ORDER

As babies
Nervously dance
To the music
Of profane phrases
A scream
A cry
She has a broken jaw
And a black eye
And he is stabbed
Repeatedly
Straight into his pride
It's gone too far
Now someone outside
Of themselves Is assigned
To solve the problem
Someone
Must get out
Die
Jail
Drop charges
Make up
Hit
Hurt
Or just stop
Just stop
Look and wake up
To SELF RESTRAINTS.

SOME CALL IT JAZZ

A note, a sound
A feeling
A beautiful melodic expression
Flowing through artist
To listener
Then back again

Some call it JAZZ

It's been categorized
Defined and analyzed
This message music
Of soul and mind
But the one who blows it
Really knows it

Some call it JAZZ

Start naming the masters
The singers, arrangers
Through which it announces
Its wonderfulness
Then
This here poem
May never end

THE WAILING
OF ROBERT NESTA MARLEY

Up from the trenchtown
On the Island
They call Jamaica
Rose a son of Africa

Said he was a born wailing
Born wailing

Said the singing
Started with him crying
Needing to be free
Then the crying
Was a moving him
To tell the righteous
Don't fear
No worry

Said the wailing
Was a gift
A message
For the brothers
For the sisters
For oppressors
All Babylon Society
Said he had to sing it
Spread it
Chant it
For the sufferah

Said he was a born wailing
Yea Mon!
Dis a Reggae Music
Rebel Music
All he wanted to do
Was

Wail a message of truth
Said it was the Jah light
Spirit within
Pushing him on through
Yea Mon
Like a mighty wind
The Irie Vibration
Blowing in the lyrics
Of a Soul Rebel

Moved over mountains
Valleys
Across water
Touching continents
Yea Mon

Spread
Like a sweet scent
This unique sound
Serenaded the people
Moved the people
Still
Make them sing together
Make them dance together
With the One Love
The One Heart

Said he was a born wailing
Born wailing
Yeh Mon
Dis a Reggae Music
Roots Music
Said he was a dreadlock Rasta
Wailing to go to Ethiopia
Calling for deliverance
Of every sufferah

Used the power of his song
Rocked the foundation
Of Babylon
Whose very children
Now in this future
Dance
To the Exodus Movement
Said no woman no cry
Yeh Mon
A natural mystic
Made him play
Emancipated melodies
Guided him
To chant proverbs
With uninhibited voice
Just a wailing
Wailing his whole soul
To the world
The Roots Rock Reggae
Yeh Mon
A soul rich with the beat
Of life's rhythm

Said he was a born wailing
Born wailing
His Redemption Songs

HE'S MY DRUMMER BROTHER
(for my brother Vincent Hall)

He's my drummer brother
   Not like no other
For his color is sound
   His color is rhythm
Which lights up
   Inner Rooms
Which Pulsates with soul

He's my drummer brother
   Not like no other
Shining and burning
   Beating a message
With every rock, roll
   And rumble of his sticks

He's my drummer brother
   Not like no other
Gently soothing, intensely grooving
   In the orchestra
      Of UNITY
He's my drummer brother
   Not like no other
   For he is song
   Marching to my heartbeat

THE BRILLIANT GIANT PAUL ROBESON

The giant stood
With his African Heritage robe
Draping his life
Which flowed
Like a river
Through passages of strife
The giant spoke
And language was a song
Titled "Eloquence"
Of words which did evoke
Visions of color and brilliance
The giant proceeded
Up the academic mountain
And with agility competed
For the touch down
Before freedom's fountain
And he sang and he sang
From the depths of his soul
Poured forth a rhythmic spring
His ebony voice
Bass and drums and baritones
Lyrical, musical, rainbow tones
Strong, rich, brave and bold
A universal note
A gift to behold
The giant marched
With workers, miners
Side by side
With people
For people
For rights denied
Then the giant stepped out
The brother stepped out
Front center stage
Giving his spirit
To characters portrayed
The giant performed
Othello emerged majestic
Intense as the night
Wearing a crown of brilliance
Of cultural insight.

BILLIE HOLIDAY

Today I heard Billie singing
Saw Billie's ballad
In the eyes of a sister
Crying satin notes
Longing to be free
And up on 125
Saw her smiling
Inside the voice
Of a woman
Standing right there
On the corner
Singing her soul
To the four winds
You know
Every time Billie sang
It was a Holiday
Lady Day
Happy day
Ever so melancholy
And her Blues
Sure was no news
To Strange Fruit
Today I heard
Billie's Bebop tune
Saw a yellow basket
Swinging in the hands
Of another generation
This joint is jumpin!
But Baby
It's a crowded room
In which very few understand
Today I heard Billie's song
Saw a gardenia
A beautiful flower
Wet droplets of joy
Pain dripping from

Community

Her petals
Touching her people still
A melody making us know
That God does Bless
The child that's got it's own
Today I heard my mother
Play one of her sides
And say
"Sing it girl!"
Billie Holiday is sharp
Sing it Billie
Yeh Baby
They treated her bad
Sing it Billie
She really dug that cat
Sing it Billie
Really loved him
Sing it Billie
Don't explain
Sing it
Ain't nobody's business
If I do
That's my girl
Sing it
They gave her that stuff
To mess her all up
Sing it Billie
Sing it.

THE RED SNOW OF SARAJEVO

All in the name of ethnic cleansing
Hatred's reason
An excuse used before
Explodes fire and ice
Its insanity spreads
Disease rolling thunder
Up and down mountains
Tidal waves of madness
Chilling Humanity
Drowning sacred life
Spilling destruction
Into an infants stroller
Blown over
Broken
Torn
Smashed
                In the red snow
                  of Sarajevo

Its severed finger
Points to the sky
Bleeds
Its mothers cry
The sound heard before
Proclaims the slaughter
Of families born despised
Bosnian, Croatian
Christian, Muslim
Human divided
By three times devil
                In the red snow
                  of Sarajevo

The fuel of war is evil
A foot separated
A body buried
Where it could not run
Could not play
Could not grow

Community

Could not laugh
Father went to market
Never to return
Caught by the mortar
Bombs, bullets, smoke
Smoke, smoke, smoke
Smoke the darkness
                In the red snow
                of Sarajevo

The world reflection
Hope longing Peace
To defrost hate
Love and happiness
Frostbitten
In the red snow
of Sarajevo

In blood, fire, ice
Blood, fire, ice
War, fire, ice
Hate, fire, ice
Crime against innocence
Barbarism
War where winners are none
Loss reigns
Number One
                In the red snow
                of Sarajevo
Consciousness must thrive
Root its prayer
Call to the Most High
To melt the
Cold atrocity.

                In the red snow
                Of Sarajevo

THIS TRANE

This Trane
Rides not on wheels
Nor tracks
    This Trane is going!

This Trane
Rolls on and on
With EXPANSIONS
Of EXPRESSIONS
Blowing all MY FAVORITE THINGS
    This Trane is floating!

This Trane
Moves fast, slow
Steady
Never bumpy
Nor even rocky
    This Trane can sing!

It screams
It shouts
A song of Praise
To the Power
Behind its locomotion
    This Trane blows and blows!

When it blows
It blows
With a breath of soul

Rolls a melody
Way on up
To the EQUINOX

This Trane
Rides not on
Wheels nor tracks

For This Trane
Is the Coltrane
John Coltrane
Traveling
With A LOVE SUPREME.

THE BURNING SPEAR
GUARDIAN OF REGGAE

The guardian of reggae
The Burning Spear
Keeper of the flame
Keeping it pure
His music endures
Winds of change
His rhythm soars
wings ignited
His song exhales
Fire of truth
His song roars
With lions awakened
His beat burns
Past to present
A future drum
In feet liberated
The real Nyabinghi
Rides through the earth
Sings with the spirit
And souls uplifted
Dancing to the fire
Fire of culture
Dancing to the water
Water of Roots
Singing in sound
The African teacher
Protector of Original
Message spiritual
His lyrics flow
Above modern shadows
His melody shines
The natural light
The guardian of reggae
The Burning Spear
Keeper of the flame
Keeping it pure.

METAMORPHOSIS

OF

LOVE

PATH

*O*n a moments notice

A train ride
By your side
Was a journey
On a soul vibe
Made me wonder
What was this thunder
Which beat like a drum
On my drum

On a moment's notice
An African son
Made me wonder
While the rhythm
Of train tracks
Carried me back
Through ancient stories
We told
And rode
Made us ponder
The vision
Something may
Possibly unfold

On a moments notice
A journey
Into a stare
Suspended
Captured
Held there

On a moments notice

A train ride
By your side
Where our words
Played music
Floated like incense
Then sweetened
The air.

Metamorphosis of Love

HONEY HUSH!

One day
He walked my way
And I just didn't know
What to do
Or say
All he did
Was give me a greeting
Told me
This was the rarest meeting
And something else
Very nice that he said
Turned the brown freckles
On my face to red
HONEY HUSH
HAVE YOU EVER SEEN
A GROWN WOMAN BLUSH?

I just couldn't look
Into his eyes
It was a bit
Of a surprise
Plus this sister
Is by no means
Fickled
But I nervously
Giggled
And I really
Tried to hide
The fact
The brother
Actually had an effect
Like that
HONEY HUSH
HAVE YOU EVER SEEN
A GROWN WOMAN BLUSH?

So I maintained
A posture of respect
Avoided his look
And the whole subject
So shy was I
Even to stare
Looked down
At my hands
And counted my carfare
Then he switched
Conversation
Started talking
About struggle
While a tone
In his voice
Made me comfortable
I lifted my eyes
He gave me a compliment

Though I was
Charmed
I fell into silence
He gave me his number
I hopped
On the bus

HONEY HUSH
HAVE YOU EVER SEEN
A GROWN WOMAN BLUSH?

THE PHONE STARTED RINGING

    The phone started ringing
      Then I knew
    The sound of singing
      Touchtones from you

    The phone started ringing
      Music did begin
    The music was the voice
      Of a sweet dear friend

    The phone started ringing
        The note bright aqua blue
    It's melody lingering
      In thoughts of you

    The phone started ringing
      then I knew
    You would like the singing
      I would like you

    The phone kept ringing
      Music did start
    The music in the voices
      Of two inspired hearts

SUNMAN

You
Come my way
It's a bright sunny day
WEATHER REPORT
Says 100 degrees
In a hot summer sun
You
Come my way
Birds suddenly
Sound like Sarah Vaughn
Like Coltrane
Playing all of our
Favorite Things
Fanning my spirit
To coolness
You
Come my way
It's a sunny
Funny day
You
Come my way
Even when Autumn leaves
Begin to play
WEATHER REPORT
Says windy and cool
But what do they know
You show
Suddenly your presence
Like a warm breeze
Moves in
With the Easterly wind
Covering me
Like a sweater
Then
There's no need
For a windbreaker
You
Come my way
 It's a bright Autumn day

Metamorphosis of Love

You
Come my way
In the coldest winter day
WEATHER REPORT
Says 10 degrees
Below zero
A snowstorm expected
Hail and sleet
You show
In a bouquet
Of snow
Then each flake
Falling
Is a crystal smile
Radiating the air

You
Come my way
On a bright Spring day
When seeds
begin to swell
And flowers
Grow like feelings
WEATHER REPORT
Says clouds
Rain, thunderstorms
Flooding
In certain areas
You show
And it's all dried
By the vibe
Blowing In the wind
You
Come my way
It's always
A bright sunny day
And
The Weatherman
Says the climate
Is like that
When THE SUNMAN
Comes around.

OUR FRIENDSHIP

It's like silk
    Soft, gentle, smooth
Wrapping our spirits
    With luminous color
It's like silk
    Intriguing, mystifying
    Captivating
Trimmed with a golden thread
    Of affection
It's like silk
    Beautiful, delicate
    Subtle
    Tender and submissive
    Yet reinforced
    With stitches of kindness
It's like silk
    Moved by the action
    Of warm wind
    Clothing our hearts
    In peaceful stillness
It's like silk
    Sensual, colorful
    Joyful to the touch
Pleasant to wear
Like a garment
Especially woven
    For us

BOUQUET

The bell rang
I answered the door
And there you were
A special delivery
Wrapped with a satin bow
Pink, red, blue
White, yellow
Nothing but color
Smiling at me
Like a rainbow
Surprising
And lighting
My face
Something wonderful
Decorating
My space.

WHY

Because you're
Just nice
Yes, I thought
About this
More than twice
You're caring
And sharing
Mostly you respect
Me
And don't stress
Or press
Me
Because your word
Is bond
And you don't
Just dance
And sing a song
Why?
Well
You're also
Spiritual
And don't act
Mean and irritable
And
You really know
How to relate
To me
With love
And solidarity
That's why
That's why

YOU

Before I closed my eyes
I opened my eyes
Opened my eyes
I had a dream about you
Dream about you
So bright
Illusive blue was it
So unforgettable
True was it
It was about you, you
All about
You presenting yourself
Before me
There you were
Standing
On the sunrise
Of my life
On the right hand of my life
Looking at me
Looking at you
Before I opened my eyes
Opened my eyes
I closed my eyes
Closed my eyes
Again
Opened my eyes
I had a dream about you
Dream about
You gently
Took my hand
Held my heart
At the edge
Of a starlit night

At the horizon
Of your life
Came in
From the battlefield
Victorious, humble
Laid down
Your weary armor
I touched the temples
Of your soul
Then Prayer was our tablecloth
Peace was our sacred breakfast
And Love was
The order of our day.

INNER VISIONS

IT'S LATER THAN WE THINK

Given a budget
From THE ONE TRUE FRIEND
Something you can't borrow
Something you can't lend
Nor even turn back
Like the hands
Of a clock
Subtract
Double
Invest like stock

Given a budget
From THE ONE TRUE FRIEND
This thing called TIME
We all must spend
SACRED is time
Motion and power
The second
To the minute
Make up the hour
The day
To the month
The month
To the year
Only a moment
The message is clear
A moment to live
A moment to grow
Inside the moment
Which has to go
It flashes on by
As fast as you blink
Check out the time
It's later
Than we think

Inner Visions

Given a budget
From THE ONE TRUE FRIEND
Who has no beginning
Who has no end
Spend it well
And then be glad
For if you don't
You'll wish you had
No matter the age
Or financial means
Time can be used
To fulfill dreams
Work to the limit
Reach for the sky
Rest a minute
Then
PRAISE THE MOST HIGH

Given a budget
From THE ONE TRUE FRIEND
Something you can't borrow
Something you can't lend
Time is the essence
It can't be banked
It doesn't show favors
To status or rank
Nor stays on hold
So you can rewind
The life
That got lost
Wasting TIME.

GIFTS AMONG MYRIADS

I awakened at dawn
And found my heart still beating
Awakened at dawn
And I was still breathing
Saw night overcome
By the light of morn
And found my two eyes
Still seeing
Thought was here
My mind still reading
A gift of living
From the Divine Being
Awakened from sleep
And found I could still talk
Another day to sow
To reap
Arose from my bed
And was blessed to walk
I awakened at dawn
By the Will of the Great
Found my body functioning
At a normal rate
And I said
    ALLAHU-AKBAR, ALLAHU-AKBAR
    ALLAH IS GREAT

I looked out into the world
And saw the sun
Still burning
Looked out across the land
And the earth
Was still turning
Breathed a deep breath
There was oxygen
In the air
I used all five senses
And found more life
Everywhere
I thirsted for a drink
And water
Was still flowing

Inner Visions

I hungered for food
Found vegetables
Fruit
Seeds still growing
And I said
    ALLAH-AKBAR, ALLAHU-AKBAR
    ALLAH IS GREAT
    ALLAH, THE ALL KNOWING
I went out into the world
Among other humans
Like me
Who each day
Awaken at dawn
And live dependently
Went out
Among those who struggle
To answer the Call
In humble prostration
Before Him
We did fall
I went out
To the masjid
With the faithful
Did pray
And together
We gave PRAISE
To THE MOST MERCIFUL
Of the day
Went out
Among the people
Where Truth
Was being heard
And found them
Still spreading
The gift of DIVINE WORD
Another chance
To be awake
Together
We all said
    ALLAHU-AKBAR, ALLAHU-AKBAR
    ALLAH IS GREAT
    ALLAH IS GREAT

CHERISH

Cherish the daylight
For it is always passing
Cherish SUPREME LOVE
For it is EVERLASTING
Cherish true friendship
For it is genuine
Cherish happiness
Peace sublime
Cherish life
Journey of soul
Cherish the moment
Which now unfolds

DREAMS

Some people go through life
Without purpose or aim
Some people go through life
In misery and pain
Some people don't have hope
Nor see a way out
And they just can't cope
Because they live with doubt
But there are those
Who just take one day at a time
They are the ones
With the positive minds
They are the ones
Who change a negative condition
They are the ones
Who possess the inner vision

So
You just need to know
You've got to act
On your dream

Inner Visions

Move on your dream
What would life be
What would life mean
Without dreams
You've got to dream
You've got to dream
What would life be
What would life mean
Without dreams.

INNER VISION

One rainy morning
Two people
Two people like me
Like you
Set out for a days work
One rainy windy morning
Looking out the cafe window
Drinking my coffee
Thinking up lines
>Two people like me like you
>Doing what they always do
>Only difference
>One has a seeing eye dog
>German shepherd at his side
>Firmly holds his briefcase
>Knows where he's going
>Knows what he must do

One windy rainy morning
Looking out the cafe window
Watching the world race by
>The other one has
>Two wandering eyes
>Looking for fireworks
>In the clouds
>While the one
>With the seeing eye dog
>Walks tall
>Takes his time
>Pauses

To straighten his collar
Buttons his raincoat
All the way down
Checks his shoelaces
Carefully
While the shepherd sits
Waiting obediently
While the shepherd stands
Guarding his side
One rainy morning
Two people like me like you
Outside the cafe window
Drinking my coffee
Thinking up lines
    And the other one
    Blindly scurries by
    Designer suit
    Hanging loose
    Chases after a morning beauty
Whose fragrance
Breezes by
The briefcase he swings
Has one latch unlocked
While he whistles
Calls
Chases her
The rain pounds
His head
The wind scatters
His confidential documents
And he trips
Over his open shoelaces
Bumping his head
Against the curb
One windy rainy morning
Just looking out
The cafe window
I'm drinking my coffee
Thinking up lines.

TRUTH

TRUTH IS REALITY
TRUTH IS MANIFEST
TRUTH IS SWEET
TRUTH IS BITTER
TRUTH IS TRIUMPHANT
TRUTH LIBERATES
TRUTH SACRIFICES
TRUTH SAVES
TRUTH IS CONCEALED
TRUTH IS REVEALED
TRUTH IS LIGHT
TRUTH IS FINAL

JOY OF GIVING

So exhilarating the feeling
Rejuvenating the spirit
Exciting is the deed
Being extended
Toward those outside oneself
Anticipating
The reaction of the recipient
Experiencing the satisfaction
Of the action of giving
Purifying
Is the feeling
And truly understanding
It is not so much the thing
Or material article itself
But the particle of love
Shown to those
Smiling on the other end
With gratitude
Deeply touched
As a result of a gift
Placed in their hands
A gift of being able
And willing to give
Knowing the sweet
Kind feeling
Flowing from one spirit
To another

AS THE WORM TURNS

No need to wonder
Nor ask why
The earth turns
It just does
All creation turns
Life turns
It just does
As the metamorphosis
Of the butterfly
As the worm turns
It is a sign
Uplifting
Elevating
Bewildering minds
Not so much
How the witness feels
Nor thinks
But just the reality
Of what we see
As the worm turns
It is a sign
A reflection
Of motion
Of time
Growth and change
Wisdom and light
That's life
As the worm turns
So does the world
And so do we.

PATTERNS

Procession of the ants
Artwork of the bee
Designs in all creation
The beauty and mystery
Lines, shades and colors
On flowers and leaves
The message of His patterns
A voice of harmony
Blueprints of nature
In earth and in sky
Reflects the signs of wisdom
For man to walk by
Stages, cycles and levels
Life of a minute cell
Within the human body
Where worlds do dwell
The natural BLESSINGS
All divinely sent
The message of HIS patterns
Breath of enlightenment

MORNING GLORIES

Morning glories
Wait for no man
They open their petals
By One Command
Waving through the day
Bowing closed at night
Rising on time
With The Light

FROM LIBERTY PARK

Where inner city anthems
Rap
To THE STAR SPANGLED BANNER
And sea gulls
Scream
Survival over polluted shores
And vegetation
Just manages
To spread out
A multicolored cloak
Lady liberty is revitalized
When mentalities have yet
To be renovated
And true freedom
Experienced
Where the rising tide
Reflects
The children of the world
Struggling for equality
Struggling To coexist.

FROM THE BEACH

How the waves
Keep coming
Landing on the shore
How humanity keeps pushing
Through life's open door
How the waves
Keep bringing
Treasures from the ocean floor
And how the TRUTH
Is manifest
More and more.

FROM THE MOUNTAIN

Looking down
Looking out
Looking up
Looking inward
Breathing
The panorama
The colorful mosaic
The mystic beauty
Of earth crowned
By wonders
And sky
All yielding
Submitting
To the rhythm
Of creation
Watching
Listening
As it exemplifies
The ESTABLISHED ORDER
Where mountains
Connect to valleys
United by ONE FORCE

Where the movement
Of streams
Within the total movement
Sing
Of one mighty waterfall
Carving trails
To flow free.

FROM NEGRIL

It is totally tranquil here
Sacred sun
Soft sand
Pristine waters
Green foliage
Flourishes with richness
Yet I realize
This was once
Another stop
The slave traders made

I'm among my people
Constantly reminded

Coral
Aqua blue
Water
It's so beautiful
Praise to its Creator
I can actually see
All the stars at night
The sun rises
And sets
So dramatically
The water calls
And I'm swimming

Cultural and crucial

Rhythms play
Down every road
While Bob Marley's music
Blows with the wind
Some call you girl
More than sister
But don't touch
Unless
It's your mission

People here
Skillfully use their hands
To the fullest
Carving
Weaving
So artistically
Make jewelry
Go about the labor of survival
Like a ritual.

THE BIRD

Such a pretty little thing
With wings so fragile
Takes to the air
Can do that razzle dazzle
My how it flies
So natural and free
Sings to the wind
A sweet soul melody
And in the early morning
Before the break of day
Welcomes the sunlight
With a song of Praise
Such a pretty little thing
Rising from the nest
Singing in the tree of life
In its tree of rest

DANCE OF THE DANDELIONS

In winter's cold
They hide
Waiting, waiting
In life's soft bed
They hide
Awake and slumbering
Waiting, waiting
For the CHOREOGRAPHER'S call
Rebelliously rising
Obediently arriving in Spring's
Sweet radiant face
Through restless wind
They rise
With gentle breeze
They grow
A yellow horizon
Of smiling eyes
In rain and sun
Dancing, dancing
With the fragrance
Of rebirth.

21,000 FEET

Strapped to my seat
Flying high
21,000 feet
In the sky
Whether it crashes
Or safely lands
All held
In the Almighty's hands
Can't see the earth
From way up here
It's worth saying
A prayer
Then down

Down, down
Down and down
Back on sacred ground

EYES ARE WINDOWS

Eyes are windows
Through which
The soul looks
Record the reflections
Not found
In paper books
Eyes are windows
Where sunlight
Shines through
And carry
Life's moisture
Like
Wet morning dew

A REMINDER

We may plan year to year
Month to month
Week to week
Day to day
In actuality
We live
Breath to breath

CONSOLATION

If the sun
Abruptly departs
After smiling
So brightly
On your soul
And clouds of darkness
Carry you off
Into the storm
Then remember
The rays
Which touched you
For one second
Have the power
To touch you
Again and again

AUTUMN AGAIN

Again summers heat
Announces its departure
With true colors revealing
A red orange rapture
As earth's little creatures
Rush to prepare
Amid leaves
Gently descending
Through crispy air

RESPECT TO THE MAX

So what do you expect
What goes around
Comes around
When you don't give
Respect to the max
There's a heavy tax
On your crown
Now London Bridge
Is falling down
What becomes
Of an inflated ego
Does the big fat balloon
Grow and grow
I don't think so
Good conquers evil
And Pop
Goes the weasel!
Off comes the veil
As real intentions
Lay unpeeled
Before the eyes
Of those victimized
Surely you must realize
When you don't give
Respect to the max
There's a heavy tax
And the actual fact
Following your track
Is that
You're not so tough
Nor even tall
Remember
Humpty Dumpty
Had a great fall
Family nor sincere friends
Couldn't help him
Pull it together again
So when you don't give
Respect to the max
Sooner or later
You face a tax

NEW BEGINNINGS

The END of something
Once so together
Seemingly falling apart
May be

The BEGINNING of something
Coming back together
Once again
Yet brand new
And even more together

USUALLY AFTER THE BRAINSTORM

It's usually after
After sweating
After searching
After what seems a test
Of endurance
Thinking so hard
Hurting
Struggling, tugging
Wrestling with a thing
Turning it over
And over
In your mind
Praying, praying
And praying
It's usually after
Experiencing the anxiety
Of a thing
The trial of a thing
Working with it
It's usually after
The brainstorm
That a ray of light
Appears
And opens the door
Leading
To the solution
Of it

THE DAYS

They flow
Like waves
One into the other
Touching the shore
Of life
Arriving, departing
Arriving, departing
Sun rising
Sun setting
Events
Like a procession
Marching down the runway
Of roses
Of thorns
Sunshine and raindrops
Rise, fall
Their harmony
Singing Truth
In perfect keys
Light and dark
They flow
Like waves
One into the other
Up and down
Over and over
Like a dance
We need to learn
A song
We need to remember
A celebration
We need to join in
Sink or swim
In the supreme program
Move in its rhythm
Get swept in the current
They flow
Like waves
One into the other
What treasures

Shall be left on the sand?
Pearls or bones?
Pearls or bones?
Happiness, grief
They flow
Blessed never the less
Tests
Until then
The ultimate question
Before the end
Answered

WINTER

Cold is the ice
Of this winter day
Cold is the season
Of its reason
Cold is the ice
Of this winter day
Wise is the sign
Of its time
When snow falls
When heat calls
Then wind
Blows emotions
Across frozen oceans
And warmth's stillness
Like dormant seeds
Await leaves crumbled
Beneath bare trees
Chilled, chilled
Chilled unto change
In earth's bosom
Rearranged
Cold, cold, cold
Cold is the ice
Cold is the ice
Cold is the ice
Of this winter day
Cold is the cold
The heat
It has sent away
There still
To burn
From its distance
There still
Longing to return
There still
To yearn
The peace of its comfort
Its feeling of ease.

RAMADAN RAPTURE

Oh Ramadan!
Your days are a mercy
To my soul
    Your fire
    Purifies my heart
    Changes to cool water
    Quenches spiritual thirst
    Nourishes my spirit
In the beginning
Middle
End of your journey
I have reached your Oasis
Tasted your humbling Reality
Rested my struggle
In the Peace
The Peace of your shade
    The Peace
    Of the Most High One

Oh Ramadan!
    The Stars
    Of all your nights
Have testified
To the Light
The Truth
Which dispels
And decorates darkness

Perseverance moves
Into Victory
Delivers reward
As a sweet delicacy

Oh Ramadan!
    I have crossed
    Your sand

Inner Visions

    Bathed
    In the Mighty Waterfall
    And waited
Waited to capture
The Ramadan Rapture

Allahu Akbar! Allahu Akbar!
Here once more
The Loving Spirit
Alhamdullilah
All Praise and Thanks
Holds me
Surrounds me
    And from this space
    I can see clearly
    From where the Master
    Has carried me
Captured, captured
By the Ramadan Rapture
Ramadan Rapture

Oh Ramadan!
Your days
Have born me abundant fruit
Prepared a Feast
Of Sweet Freedom.

I'M JUST A POEM

I'm just a poem
Walking, talking
Writing
Sharing my thoughts
Things I see
Things I feel
Inspiring me
I'm just a poem
Reacting
Expressing this time
In which I live
A mere moment
To give
Vibrations of love
All I have is a poem
I'm just a poem
All I have left
Is a poem
A poem

WATER

It moves me
Beyond the desert city
For I am it
While something of bone
Something of flesh
Yet I am more
Of it
Circulating, pulsating
Through my very system
It is the life
It is the milk
It is the red blood
The crystal spring
The salty sea
The liquid murky river
It moves me
To drink waterfronts
Where I sit
In thoughts that float
Raining sentimental tears
Into its comforting ripples
Rising with joy
Laughter rides the crests
Of each foamy wave
Overwhelmed
I then weep
Weep the moment
Diving into beauty
It moves me
In deliverance of realization
Be still my heart
Be still and listen
The sun, moon and stars
In concert with water
Speak balance
While the shore recites

Existence
Something constantly coming
Coming, coming
Something going far
Far away
Toward remembrance
Into expansive distance
The horizon
A line between
The seen and the unseen
Where my ship
My -life navigates
The water
It moves me
Truely
I am of it
Where I sit
Throwing my pebbles
Into splashes of Truth
Submerging my body
Into the wetness
From which I am
Created.

May 19, 1996

It's in the 80's
Thank you Lord!

Never saw a May
Like this one

So Chilly, so windy
So rainy
Weatherman said one thing
The Almighty said another
The signs came down
Like hailstones
Big as grapefruit

Yet flowers grew
Their colors of submission

But did we?

My body shocked
Longed to shed
My leather
Landlord shut off heat
Early in April
It's a housing thing ·
Again May came
This spring
Cold and hot
Followed your command

Moved in a rhythm
I never saw before

They wore short sleeves
Then shivered in forty degrees
A big surprise!
Praise, thanks
A lesson heard
Loud and clear

"You can't appreciate the warmth If you've never felt the cold."

May 19, 1996
I just want to shout
Chant down the negative
Ingratitude
I want to jump up
Change attitude
Dance a spirit dance
Walk barefoot
Wear feathers, beads
And cowry shells
I want to dance
In Olatunji's Drums of Passion
Rise like the sun
Sprout like a seed
Fly like a bird

Then sit quietly down
Peacefully down
In this field called life
Look up at the sky
In Sacred Meditation
Reflect
Write down this poem
From the main source
Where my spirit soars
Like an eagle

I want to sing
Like a crow
May 19, 1996
Let people know
Wisdom moves
Through the elements

Give thanks And Feel the Power!

Inner Visions

About the Author

Writing poetry since the age of 13 Ameerah Hasin Ahmad, recipient of The Paul Robeson Award was born and raised in Jersey City, New Jersey
Poet, storyteller and playwright has made numerous appearances throughout the metropolitan area. Has appeared at various poetry spots in New York City, University of the Streets, The Nuyorican Cafe, Cafe Creole and The Moon Cafe in Brooklyn. She was featured on several cable TV programs in New Jersey. She dramatized one of her poems "Double Dutch Sister" in Newark Writers Collective's play "If The Truth Be Heard, Let It Be Told" at Newark Symphony Hall. She has performed storytelling and poetry for the Community Awareness Series sponsored by the J.C. Public Library. Presently a member of the Poetry Collective "Lucid Dreams"
She became a member of CAP, (Community Arts Program) a jazz and poetry series. Ameerah continues to edutain and inspire her listeners.

Butterfly Reflections
(201) 860-6888